Korean Mythology

Folklore and Legends from the Korean Peninsula

Table of Contents

Introduction

Myths, legends, and folklore are more than incredible and magical stories and tales. They have a profound purpose in the human world. They explain how human beings perceived and tried to understand how our world operated. Myths give us insight into the working of the human mind from ancient times. Myths are timeless and offer guidance and solutions to many of our problems and misunderstandings.

Korean mythology is a vast collection of folktales and legends from all over the Korean Peninsula. Two of the oldest existing books holding historical records of these mythological stories and tales are:

- Samguk Yusa

- Samguk Sagi

The stories and events in these two books are based on tales passed down through generations through oral tradition and lost texts. Samguk Yusa was written in the 13th century by a Buddhist monk named Iryeon. It is replete with supernatural stories and contains the myth surrounding the founding of Gojoseon or the first kingdom of the Korean people. Gojoseon is now believed to have been a real kingdom that existed during the Bronze Age. The Samguk Yusa also contains fables and tales from later periods.

Written by a Confucian scholar, the Samguk Saki is more factual than the Samguk Yusa. It lists the founding myths of the Three Kingdoms of Korea, Silla, Goguryeo, and Baekje. The author, however, tells the readers "Not to believe" these tales because they are only tales with little or no historical approval of actually having taken place. Korean mythology is drawn from the three major religions of Asia, which are Taoism, Buddhism, and Hinduism.

Other than the above two ancient texts, many more books were written documenting the Korean peninsula's myths, legends, and folklore.

Chapter 1: Important Deities in Korean Mythology

Korean mythology and folklore is full of gods, goddesses, and deities, drawn from the rich heritage of the primary belief systems. Known as "Shin," which means deity or spirit, they are supernatural beings endowed with the power to influence the human world. Shins are served by female shamans known as Mudang, especially during Gut or sacred rituals. Each god is given responsibility for a special area, although these vary depending on which version of the myth is being told. For example, in some versions, the goddess of birth is Samshin-Halmang, while in other versions, she is Danggeum-aegi.

The intensity of power and hierarchical strength also varies from god to god. To give you an example, guardians of homes are less powerful than gods of nature. Let us look at some of the important deities in Korean mythology.

The Heavenly Emperor

This deity is known by various names, including Hwanin, Hanuelmin, Sang-je, Cheonwang, and Cheonjiwang (all of which translate to "Heavenly Ruler") the ruler of the heavens. Other names include Sangje, Sanjenim (both translate to the highest emperor).

He is often compared to the Jade Emperor because of the similarity of their roles and is called Okhwangsangje or the "Great Jade Emperor. Hwanin oversees both gods and humans and, at times, can bestow divinity on a mortal and make him or her a god or goddess.

Hwanung

Hwanung was the son of Hwanin and is the god of laws. He is one of the founder-gods of Korea, especially according to the folklore of Northern Korea. Hwanung wanted to live among human beings. He told his father about this desire. Hwanin agreed to his son's request and allocated Mount Taebaek to Hwanung to establish his kingdom. Hwanin's son descended to the human world with the goddess of rain, Aryongjong, and the goddess of wind, Yondung.

With his first 3000 followers, he established the Divine City, which became his capital, and it was from here his reign spread all across Korea. He constituted all necessary laws for a civilized world in government, morality, agriculture, etc. He also laid down moral codes concerning illnesses, science, lifespans. He played an essential role in the cosmogony story in Korean mythology.

Haemosu

He is the god of the Sun and the first son of Hwanin, the Heavenly Ruler. Ancient illustrations depict him as a young man wearing a headdress made of crow feathers. All crows, specifically three-legged crows, represent the sun in many Asian cultures. Haemosu carries the Yonggwanggeom (Sword of Dragon's Light) and rides a chariot named Oryeonggeo, pulled by five dragons.

Haemosu's solar sword was his primary weapon, and it shone as brightly as the sun. As the sun went across the sky, Haemosu rode his chariot towards the earth every morning. His dragons could pull the chariot faster than the wind, and he did not travel alone; he was accompanied by a large retinue who rode white swans. As they traveled the soft floating clouds, music was heard.

Haemosu and his retinue held court in Puyeo, his capital, until sunset, after which he rode back to his solar home. Haemosu established the Buyeo Kingdom and had a son named Go-Jumong, who later established the Goguryeo

Kingdom. Interestingly, Go-Jumong conquered the Buyeo Kingdom.

Sanshin Halmang

She is the goddess of life. Halmang was once a human being and was bestowed with divinity becoming a goddess when she won a flower blooming contest. In Korean mythology, flowers symbolize life. She also shares the responsibility to protect pregnant women and babies with another goddess. As a result, she is known as the patron of midwives. Halmang protects babies and pregnant women from harm. It is believed that midwives become spirits called Samshin when they die and help Halmang in her duties.

Halmang is the patron goddess of Jeju Island and is depicted embodying the entire earth. Thanks to her magical prowess, Halmang can take on the form of a giantess and can roam the entire island naked. Most of the stories told about her tell of her nakedness. Once, she had diarrhea after consuming millet porridge, and 360 hills and mountains in Jeju Island were formed because of this malady.

The goddess also organized the valleys and rivers of the island. It is believed that her urine formed the channel connecting Jeju Island to the Korean mainland. The channel formed thus connected Jeju Island and Udo Island in some versions.

One day, the people of Jeju Island requested her to cover her nakedness. She promised them that if they could make clothes fit her gigantic size, she would build a bridge to the mainland. The people started the task of stitching garments for their giant goddess. Despite using all the fabric available on the island, they could not make clothes large enough to cover her body entirely. So, the goddess also went back on her promise and left the bridge half-finished.

There is another interesting story about Halmang and her husband, Halubang. She outdid her husband in a fishing contest and ate all the fish in the ocean through her vagina. Her husband used these fish to spawn the three progenitor gods, Koeulla, Puella, and Yangeull, who established the Three Clans of Jeju Island.

Yeongdeung Halmang

Yeongdeung Halmang, the Korean goddess of the wind and sea, visits Jeju Island once every year during the liminal period between the spring and winter seasons. She roars in from the sea as she enters the island at a village named Hansu. She usually makes an entry on the first day of the second lunar month. After a fortnight of whirling around Jeju Island furiously, she leaves, going back into the sea at Udo.

This moody goddess carries the seedlings of marine animals, plants, and other life forms. If she is in a happy mood, she spreads the seeds over the waters of Jeju Island. She is associated with dolphins who accompany her everywhere she goes. It is considered an auspicious sign if people see dolphins frolicking happily in the sea.

As she leaves Jeju Island after her annual two-week visitation, she calls out to the northwest wind and indicates her mood to the people. If there is warm weather when she leaves, she is happy. Consequently, the impending harvest is expected to be plentiful. If the weather is cold at the time of her departure, then fishermen and divers must be careful because it is an omen of impending doom.

For various reasons, worshiping Halmang is usually considered a tricky business in Korean mythology. Firstly, she is not available for worship throughout the year like the other gods and goddesses. She makes an appearance only for two weeks a year. Secondly, since she has not lived among human beings, she does not have any kind of special relationship with people, which is evident in her capricious and unpredictable nature. So, pleasing and worshiping Halmang is considered a necessary evil and is not always done with loving devotion.

Jumong

Jumong is credited with establishing the ancient Goguryeo kingdom. The present name Korea has its roots in this ancient name. His mother was Yuhwa, the youngest daughter of Haebaek. The story of Jumong and how he established one of the ancient Three Kingdoms of Korea is described in detail in another chapter in this book.

Sanshin Ryeong

Sanshin Ryeong translates to the mountain god, and every mountain in Korea is associated with a god. Typically, mountain gods are depicted as wise old men sporting flowing beards. A tiger accompanies each mountain god, and they live deep inside mountain caves, often making an appearance in shrines (or Sadangs) situated at the base of most mountains.

When they are seen in shrines, Sanshin Ryeongs listen to and answer people's prayers and wishes. Most often, lumberjacks, timber workers, and hunters pray to mountain gods seeking permission to cut down trees or hunt animals for their needs. Mountain gods are tasked with protecting nature and generally are male, although there are a few mountain goddesses. For example, Mago-halmi is the Sanshin Ryeong of Mount Jiri. Later in this book, an additional chapter is dedicated to mountain spirits and gods.

Chilseongsin

This name refers to the seven gods of the Great Dipper who bless people with longevity and good fortune. For this reason, Chilseongsin is the most worshiped divinity in Korea, and their history goes back to the Bronze age. Chilseongsin is mostly depicted as seven brothers, all attired in monk's clothing (for this reason, they are often referred to as the Seven Buddhas) or in government uniforms. In some versions, they are four sisters and three brothers, and in some others, they are shown as seven sisters.

Jang Seol-ryong was a nobleman married to eSong Seol-ryong. After many years of being childless, they had a daughter after worshiping in a temple of Buddha. One day, when she was alone, a monk impregnated the daughter. The angry parents punished their daughter by putting her into a large chest and setting it afloat in the sea.

The chest drifted away and reached Jeju Island, where she tried to come ashore. But the village gods prevented her from entering Jeju Island or any other island inhabited by human beings. Finally, the chest reached Hamdeok Village, where fishermen opened it. They saw that the girl and her babies had transformed into seven snakes. The villagers of Hamdeok also turned them away, calling them ugly, dirty creatures, and were collectively called Chilseong.

Angry at being abandoned and being called ugly, Chilseong brought bad luck to the village. The villagers began to worship Chilseong as Josang, their ancestral spirit in fear. The fishermen and divers who worshiped Chilseong were rewarded with large catches and plenty of treasures and riches.

When the villagers saw that Chilseong was rewarding people, they abandoned their village guardian deity, Seomulhalmang, and all of them prayed only to Chilseong. Seomulhalmang, angered, decided to persecute Chilseong for this. The Seven Stars fled from Hamdeok Village, but wherever they tried to find refuge, they were harassed, forcing them to flee again.

Finally, they found shelter with the Song family, who worshiped them as their ancestor deity. Chilseong, in turn, made the Song family very rich and prosperous. After their deaths, Chilseong was worshiped in Jeju Island as a single deity.

Gameunjang-Aegi

She is the goddess of good luck and fate and is also known as Samgong. She was the third daughter of a couple who eked out a living as beggars. Thanks to this daughter's ability to attract good luck, the beggar family suddenly became very rich. Driven by egos, she was thrown out of her family home, after which she married a humble man who became one of the richest men in the kingdom.

She soon found out that her parents had lost all their money, their sight and returned to begging again to make ends meet. She helped restore her parents' good luck with her magical powers. After her death, Gameunjang-aegi became the goddess of fate and good luck.

Gataekshin

These deities are the guardians of houses. People offer them food in return for good fortune and improved destiny. According to Korean mythology, the Gataekshin belonged to one big family but were all killed for various reasons and in different ways, eventually becoming divine beings associated with the guardianship of household items and homes.

For example, a concubine from the big family hanged herself in the bathroom and became a Gataekshin named Cheukshin, the guardian of restrooms and bathrooms. Gataekshin also protects houses from evil spirits, diseases, and premature death. Interestingly, it is believed that these guardians of homes and household items leave the premises when the people living in the homes become wicked or disrespect them.

Mireuk and Bucheo

These two divinities are the Korean mythological version of Maitreya and Buddha. Buddhism is widespread in Korea, and therefore, it is no surprise that Buddhist divinities find a place in Korean mythology.

Seokga

Seokga is the trickster god. He was a rebel too. It is believed that he created the human world, together with Mireuk. In Korea, Seokga is also used to refer to Siddhartha Gautama or Sakyamuni, another name for Buddha.

Yongwang

These are dragon lords and live in seas, rivers, and lakes. They are important to farmers as they rule the aquatic world and control the weather. They can transform into human beings and mate with them. Wang Geon, the founder of the Goryeo dynasty, was the son of the Yongwang of the Western Sea.

Yeomra-Daewang

His name translates to King Yeomra the Great. He was the first person to encounter death and went on to become the supreme ruler of the underworld. His role was to pass judgment on human beings and mete out appropriate punishment.

Igong

This is the deity who tended to the "Flower Garden of Life and Death" and is also known as Hallakkungi. The flowers in this special garden are the souls of all human beings. Igong oversees the quality and length of each person's life through tending the flowers. When a person's lifetime ends, Igong plucks out the relevant flower from the garden. This deity also determines the soul's rebirth status after studying the quality of life they led. Igong is hugely revered in Jeju Island.

Tangun

Tangun is believed to have been the founding deity of the Choson Kingdom which came into being around 2300 BCE. He built it where present-day Pyongyang is. Tangun was Hwanung's son. Tangun had both priestly and kingly duties. After his death, he became the god of Mount Taebaek.

Habaek

He is the god of the Yalu River, which runs between North Korea and China. Therefore, Habaek is the watch guard of the northern frontiers of Korea. You can read more about him in the story of his daughter, Yuhwa.

Yuhwa

Yuhwa was the daughter of Habaek. Haemosu, the sun god, desired Yuhwa to be his own. So, he conjured a gigantic copper palace in front of Yuhwa's house. She and her two sisters were awed by the sudden appearance of this beautiful palace. They went in and were entertained by Haemosu's attendants. When the girls were giddy with laughter and happiness at the entertainment, the palace gates were bolted and the three goddesses trapped inside.

Yuhwa's sisters managed to escape, but she got caught by Haeamosu, who took her and forced her to be his wife. He compelled her to flow through the channels that he drew on the ground. Her father, Habaek, was furious with the sun god and complained to Hwanin, who ordered Haemosu to make peace with Habaek.

Habaek and Haemosu had fought a duel in which each of them metamorphosized into a different animal. When Haemosu transformed into a carp, Haemosu took on the shape of an otter and gave chase to the carp. Haebaek turned into a deer; Haemosu took the form of a wild dog and chased the deer. Haebaek then transformed into a pheasant, and in response to this, Haemosu became a hawk and attacked the pheasant.

In this way, Haemosu won this duel easily because he was able to transform into a range of land, sea, and air animals that Habaek could not match. Habaek accepted defeat but requested a formal wedding ceremony with his daughter from Haemosu, who readily agreed.

But Yuhwa was unhappy with the forced marriage and continued to look for ways to escape. Finally, she escaped and hid in King Keumwa of Puyeo's kingdom, where she delivered Jumong, her and Haemosu's son.

Kimsuro

According to Korean mythology, the Kaya region was ruled by nine elders, each of them in charge of one of the nine city-states. There was no central authority to keep these nine rulers united. So, they prayed to Hwanin to send someone who would rule over the entire Kaya region to unite the nine city-states.

Hwanin spoke from the heavens when he heard their prayer in a loud, sonorous voice. He asked everyone to assemble near Kuji Mountain. When hundreds of thousands of people gathered, Hwanin instructed them to sing Kujiga, an ancient Korean poem.

When the song ended, Hwanin lowered a huge chariot containing six golden eggs, and Kimsuro and his five subordinates hatched from these eggs. Within a few days, all six of them grew nine feet tall. Under Kimsuro's authority, Kaya united and defeated Talhae, the god who later established the Shilla kingdom. Kimsuro was married to Hwangok, who was brought from India.

Koenegito

He was the son of Sochogunk, the shrine god of Jeju Island, and a mortal woman, Paek Chunim.

Keonegito was an uncontrollable and difficult child and high on energy. Once, when he was three years old, he was so uncontrollable that his father locked him in a chest and threw it into the sea. But Keonegito escaped from his prison and married the youngest daughter of the dragon lord of the sea.

The dragon lord had no option but to exile his son-in-law. His insatiable appetite was emptying the dragon's large larder leaving everyone starving. So, Koenegito and his wife found their way to Chonja. Here, he helped the king and the people of Chonja by chasing away a large army that was trying to invade them from the north. Being successful at saving Chonja, Koenegito became a hero.

Next, Koenegito decided to go back to Jeju Island and wreak vengeance on his parents for throwing him out into the sea. He used fear to kill them and turned his father into a mountain ridge. His mother became a shrine. Koenegito had a couple of powerful tools to help him win these and many other victories. He had a magical bronze gong. If he struck this gong once, a million soldiers would appear out of thin air. If he struck it twice, the soldiers would disappear.

Koeulla, Pueulla, and Yangeullao

These deities are the progenitor gods of Jeju Island's three clans. They are always mentioned together. They emerged from the ground, the womb of Halmang, the goddess of Jeju Island, at Mohung near Mount Chu. Even today, this spot referred to as the Hollow of the Three Clans is considered a sacred landmark in Jeju Island.

After they emerged from their mother's womb, the three brothers roamed through the kingdom, hunting animals for meat and using the skin for their clothes. When it was time for marriage, the King of Pyongyang sent three brides from mainland Korea for the three brothers.

The brides brought with them horses, calves, and the Five Grains to Jeju Island. In Korea, the Five Grains, included barley, rice, soybean, millet, and foxtail millet, represent the entirety of agriculture. Koeulla, Pueulla, and Yangeulla took a bride and established Jeju Island's Three Clans. All the people of Jeju Island to this day believe that they all descend from one of these three gods.

Chapter 2: Important People Who Became Deities

In addition to gods and goddesses, many human beings played big roles in Korean mythology. Let us look at some of them and their stories in this chapter.

Bari-Degi

Also called Bari, the translation of this name is "abandoned child." Bari was abandoned by her parents because they were disappointed that she was not a boy. She was then adopted and raised by a kind, elderly couple. She learned the truth about her biological parents when she was 15 years old.

Her birth parents were punished for the cruel act of abandoning their daughter and they both contracted a fatal illness. However, Bari was not angry with her parents. Instead, she journeyed to the Afterlife (known as Seocheon in Korean mythology) to find a cure for them.

The journey to Seocheon was long and arduous, and she had to conquer many obstacles, including unfriendly, harmful ghosts and demons. Finally, disguised as a boy, she reached the place of the Water of Life. However, the guardian of the waters said he would only allow her to take the water if she married him. Bari agreed to the proposal, married the guardian of the water of life, and bore him three sons.

After a few years, Bari's family returns to her kingdom, where she learns that her parents had died and funeral rites were being held. Despite being devastated at this news, she acted quickly and used the power of the Water of Life and Revival Flowers, which she brought from Seocheon to revive her parents. And as the myth has it, she lived a long and happy life with her family.

She became a divine being, a goddess to guide the dead to the Afterlife when she died. Bari is considered to be the first Mudang, the shamanic priestess who assists gods and goddesses in their rituals. The song of her life is highly revered among Mudangs.

Daebyeol Wang and Sobyul Wang

These were the sons of Hwanin (also known as Cheonjiwang), the Ruler of Heaven. They were also called Great Star and Small Star. They were responsible for killing one sun and one moon, thereby reducing the effect of the intense heat and cold during the day and night, from two suns and two moons. These two sons of Hwanin also killed the evil Sumyeong-Jangja.

As the story goes, Daebyeol was always better than Sobyul, which made the latter jealous of his brother. To be seen as better than his brother, Sobyul cheated in a flower-blooming contest so that he could become the ruler of the human world. After a time of feeling extremely bitter and resentful, Daebyeol forgave his brother for his error in judgment and went down to the underworld to rule it alongside King Yeomra. Together they rewarded good people and punished the bad. The story of these two brothers is detailed in the chapter dealing with Korean cosmogony myths.

Gangrim-Doryeong

This strong and brave human warrior was tasked with bringing King Yeomra to Earth to help solve the mystery of the deaths of three warriors. With the help of his clever wife, Gangrim-Doryeong traveled to Seocheon and captured the Supreme Ruler of the underworld. He then took over the leadership of Jeoseung-saja, who were the messengers from the underworld. Gangrim-Doryeong is considered to be the leader of all Jeoseung-sajas.

Jacheongbi

This peasant girl plays an important role in the myth of Jeju Island, South Korea's largest island. A divine youth named Mun-doryeon came down from the heavens to learn about Earth and humans. Jacheongbi fell in love with Mun-doryeon but pretended not to.

To spend more time with him, she disguised herself as a boy and for three years, she studied in a boys' school with him. Mun-doryeong had no idea that his friend was none other than the beautiful girl he saw the first time he landed on Earth, and when she finally revealed her true persona to him, he also confessed his love for her.

But their relationship was in jeopardy because both their families opposed it. Man-doryeong was forced to return to his heavenly home. On the other hand, she did not give up on their relationship. Jacheongbi traveled to heaven after successfully overcoming multiple obstacles and difficult encounters; she reached Mun's home. His family accepted her, and she was made the goddess of the Earth and farming.

Korean mythology is rife with stories in which human beings who performed great and heroic tasks, survived great difficulties, or genuinely repented for their mistakes were given divine status.

Chapter 3: Korean Cosmogony Myths

There are multiple versions of the creation history according to Korean mythology. We shall look at a couple of these stories in this chapter. Before the beginning, the world did not exist. Then, Goddess Mago and Yulryeo, a female deity, made an appearance. However, Yulryeo died. Mago brought forth two goddesses, Gunghi and Sohi. Each of these two female deities gave birth to two Men and Two Women of Heaven, who, in turn, created more Heavenly People.

When heaven was well-populated, Yulryeo was revived from the dead, and together they created the Earth and oceans. The Heavenly People lived in a fortress called Magoseong and ruled over all forms of life in the world. Magoseong was named in honor of the first goddess who had ever existed. Youlreyo's body became the world, and Mego lived with her.

The Birth of Human Beings

Four male divine beings guarded the four cardinal directions:

- Hwanggung and Cheonggung - Born to Gunghi.

- Hukso and Baelso - Born to Sohi.

These Heavenly Men married the four Heavenly Women and went on to have 12 children, who became the ancestors of human beings. These 12 ancestors were pure beings who drank nothing but the Earth's milk that sprang from inside Magoseong, the heavenly fortress. They all possessed huge powers. They could act without seeing, talk without using words, and be almost immortal because their lifespan extended to ten thousand years.

Then came a time when the population increased so much that there was not enough of the Earth's milk to go around for everyone. A man named Jiso from Baekso's lineage was so starved one day that he decided to kill himself instead of suffering from hunger. He started climbing a cliff, and on his journey, he saw grapes growing from the earth of the cliff. In his intolerable hunger, he started eating the grapes. This incident, known as the Incident of Five Tastes, is how human beings came to have the sense of five tastes, including sourness, sweetness, spiciness, bitterness, and saltiness.

Happy to have survived, Jiso returned to his people and told them about his discovery. Considering that there was not enough of the Earth's Milk for everyone, more people started eating the grapes. However, very soon, they ate another living being to survive and as a result began to grow teeth and venomous saliva.

These people began to see but could not hear the sounds of the heavens anymore. They became impure, with their skin coarse and their feet very heavy. These impure beings' lifespan reduced drastically, and they began producing animal-like offspring. Seeing the catastrophic events, the people of Magoseong began to blame Jiso and exiled him and his entire lineage from the heavenly fortress.

Feeling sympathy for them, Hwanggung offered an alternative. He told Jiso and the people from his line that if they found a way to regain their pure forms, then they could stay behind and be freed from their misery. The impure beings were determined that the only way they could regain their pure form was by drinking Earth's milk again.

To do this, they stormed into the heavenly fortress, took it over, and razed it, hoping to find the source of the spring of Earth's milk. But, instead, something terrible happened. The milk started flowing in all directions and turned into hard, inedible earth. Now, Jiso's people and everyone who lived in the heavenly fortress were starving.

A massive famine followed this catastrophic event driving people to eat not only the forbidden grapes but all other plants and animals they could lay their hands on to survive and feed their hunger. In this mayhem, only Hwanggung approached Mago, begging for forgiveness for everyone. He took it upon himself to do everything in his power to restore human beings to their pure form.

Mago gave him three Heavenly Heirlooms and Great Knowledge. Hwanggung gathered all the people together and taught them the art of agriculture. He then handed over the Heirlooms to three leaders and sent them to earth to populate it.

Cheonggung was sent to the east to set up China. Beakso took his people to the west and established the Middle East and Europe. Huko and his people went to the south and set up the lands that are present-day Southeast Asian countries. Hwanggung and his group of three thousand people went to the north, a bitterly cold and dangerous place called Cheonsanju or "the land of the heavenly mountain."

Hwanggung deliberately chose this place because he believed a difficult life would rejuvenate his pure state, and he also swore a terrible oath that he would recover his purity.

The Heavenly Heirloom he brought from the Heavens gave him and his people power over the sun and the fire element. With this, he was able to rule strongly for a thousand years. And he was able to become pure once again.

Hwanggung had three sons. He handed over the Heavenly Heirloom to Yuin, his eldest son, giving him the right to rule over the entire kingdom. He gave his younger two sons one province each, after which he retired to the Heavenly Mountain, where he became a permanent stone through which Yulryeo delivered her messages to the human world. These messages resonated with the importance of leading a life of righteousness, purity, and innocence.

Yuin ruled over the northern kingdom for a thousand more years. He taught his people how to tame fire and how to cook food. When it was time, he handed over the Heavenly Heirloom to his son named Han-in (also spelled as Hwan-in). Han-in was the last Heavenly ruler. He used the Heirloom to attract plenty of sunlight to his kingdom, and he ruled over it well for another thousand years. Therefore, with 3000 years of excellent rule under Hwanggung, Yuin, and Han-in, people lost their animal-like features and recovered their human appearance.

Founding of Gojoseon

According to Korean mythology, the god responsible for the formation of Korea was Hwanung, who lived in the heavens. He was the third son of Hwanin, the Heavenly Emperor. Hwanung approached his father one day and expressed concern for the humans of the earth. He told his father that he wanted to rule over them to benefit all earth people.

This concept is referred to as "Hongik-Ingan," which translates to "widely benefit the human world." In fact, "Hongik-Ingan" is present-day South Korea's national motto. Emperor Hwanin agreed to send his son to earth along with a few divine beings and elements, including:

- Cheonbu-Samin - The Three Heavenly Seals.

- Three thousand servants from the heavens.

- The Gods of Wind, Cloud, and Rain.

The Three Heavenly Seals represent tokens of rulership and include:

- The divine mirror, singyeong, which stands for sovereignty over a group of people. The divine mirror represented by a bronze mirror is found in the tombs of ancient Korean tribal chiefs.

- The divine sword, singeom, stands for military commandership and is the sword of the king.

- The divine drum (singo) is used in sacred rituals to call upon the gods to report human affairs to them. Sometimes, the divine drum is replaced by the divine rattle, silyeong.

Hwanung, accompanied by all the above heavenly gifts from his father, descended down to earth and first landed on the peak of Mount Taebaek, where he founded a city called "Shinshi," or the City of the Gods. Hwanung took on the responsibility of 360 human-related works such as agriculture, justice, sickness, good and evil, and more.

When Hwanung was getting the human world ready, a bear and a tiger came to him wishing to become humans. Hwanung wanted to test their determination and spirit. So, he gave them each a handful of mugwort and 20 garlic cloves and said, "You should live in an isolated, extremely dark, sunlight-deprived cave for 100 days with nothing more to eat but the mugwort and garlic cloves I have given you. If you survive this test, then I will make you humans."

The tiger did not pass the test and ran away very soon after the ordeal began. The bear, however, passed the test with flying colors. She waited patiently. On the 21st day, Hwanung gave in to her forbearance and turned her into a beautiful lady. She was named Ungnyeo or Bear-Woman.

Soon after turning into a woman, Ungnyeo began longing for a child of her own. She prayed every day under the Divine Altar Tree, Sindansu, for a child. But there wasn't another human who could marry her and with whom she could have a child. So, to appease Ungnyeo's desire, Hwanung transformed himself into a human being and helped Ungnyeo deliver a baby boy named Dangun Wanggeom. Dangun Wanggeom is believed to be the forefather of all Korean people.

Dangun established a new kingdom called Asadal, or "the place of the shining morning sun." Asadal's name was changed to Joseon, and he set up his capital at Pyongyang Fortress. This Joseon was later changed to Gojoseon, which means "Ancient Joseon," to distinguish it from the new Joseon Kingdom, which was established later. When Dangun was 1908, he left the human world and became a Mountain God or "Sanshin Ryeong."

How the World Was Created - The Hamheung Version

According to Korean mythology another version of how the world was created is the story that includes Miruek, a divine being discussed in an earlier chapter. According to this version, Miruek placed four strong copper pillars between the earth and sky and parted the world. Until this time, the earth and the sky were stuck together. At this time, the world had two suns and two moons.

Mireuk took one of the two suns and created the constellations of Ursa-Major, the Seven-Star Dipper of the North, along with other stars. He took one of the two moons and created Sagittarius, the Seven-Star Dipper of the South, and other stars. He then wove hemp from arrowroot vines and made himself a monk's robe.

A mouse helped him discover fire and water. The mouse told him to climb Mount Geumjeong, where he was to strike a stone against pig iron to get fire. For water, Mireuk climbed Mount Soha, where he found a spring. In return for its help,

Miruek gave all the barns of the world to the mouse.

He then created human beings from five golden and five silver bugs. The silver bugs became women, and the golden bugs became men. He made the first set of clothes from kudzu vines. Miruek's world faced a challenge for power the deity, Seokga, who challenged him to three contests.

The first contest involved stretching a rope across the Sea of Japan. Seokga's silver rope broke while Miruek's golden rope helped him win the first contest. The second contest was that the deities had to connect the Seongcheon River with all the other rivers in the universe. Mireuk won this contest also by calling winter ice for help.

In the third contest, the deities grew a magnolia flower. When the deities slept, the flower that reached out to would be the winner. The flower reached out to Mireuk. But the resentful Seokga cut the magnolia and put it in his own lap. This act angered Mireuk, and he cursed the earth with numerous imperfections, including betrayal, prostitution, boastfulness, mental illnesses, etc. Soekga imprisoned Mireuk for this act.

Mireuk spent only three days in prison, after which he escaped by transforming himself into a musk deer. Seokga along with 3000 priests, followed Miruek and killed him. He ate the musk deer's flesh and shared it with the priests. All but two of the priests ate the meat. The two who did not follow Seokga's orders were turned into a stone and a pine tree. To this day, people eat flower pancakes (hwajeon in Korean) in honor of the murdered priests.

How the World Was Created - The Jeju Island Version

Before the beginning of the world, there was nothing but emptiness. One day, a gaping hole formed in this void. The lighter elements rose from the hole and formed the sky. The heavy elements fell down into the hole and formed the earth. Next, a blue dewdrop fell from the sky, and a black dewdrop rose from the earth. When these two dewdrops merged, all forms of existence, the stars, sun, and moon, came to being. Humans and even gods came from the mixing of these two dewdrops.

The leader of the gods was Cheonjiwang, and he awoke into existence at the crowing of three roosters:

- The Rooster Emperor of the Sky.

- The Rooster Emperor of the Earth.

- The Rooster Emperor of Human Beings.

The crowing or the cry of the three roosters signify the beginning of time. The leader of the gods realized the three roosters were crowing and crying because there was no sun. He then created two suns and two moons. The two suns rose and set every day, and the moons rose and set every night.

The leader of human beings was Sumyeong Jangja. He was the first person to tame wild beasts. He ruled the human world with the help of his nine horses, nine bloodhounds, and nine bulls. He took away all the crops that the humans reaped, leaving behind just enough so that they didn't starve.

Sumyeong Jangja proudly rode a golden chariot drawn by his nine horses and surrounded by the nine powerful bloodhounds, and with all this power, he became invincible. His vanity reached such great heights that he hollered to the universe, "there is no one in this world who can subdue me!"

Hearing these words, the leader of the gods, Cheonjiwang, got furious. His army of gods thundered in anger. They decided to invade

Sumyeong's kingdom. Cheongijwang rode on his golden chariot, drawn by five gigantic dragons. His powerful lieutenants included:

- General Lightning.

- General Thunder.

- General Fire.

- The Masters of Rain and Wind.

Each of the four generals had an army of 10,000 warriors. When Cheonjiwang and his huge armies reached Sumyoeng's palace, he climbed a willow tree and shouted, "Foolish and vain Sumyeong, come and kneel before me."

Instead of obeying the deity's orders, Sumyeong sent his horses, beasts, and bulls to Cheonjiwang. But, with a simple wave of his hand, the leader of the gods magically transported them to the terrace of Sumyeong's palace. Another wave of Cheonjiwang's hands and the iron pots in the kitchen launched themselves into the palace gardens.

Finally, Sumyeong Jangja came out and fought bravely against the deities and their armies. But, in the end, he was defeated and had to kneel before Cheonjiwang. The divine leader put an iron ring on the human king's head, and he howled in pain as his head seemed to explode. But nothing could get the ring out of his head. The final act of desperation to relieve himself from the excruciating pain was to order one of his slaves to decapitate him so that his suffering would end.

Hearing this brave decision, Cheonjiwang finally gave in and removed the ring from Sumyeong's head. But, instead of returning to heaven, the leader of the Gods (who had acute hearing powers) decided to spend the night at Grandmother Baekju's cottage. There, he heard a girl brush her hair with a jade comb. The girl was Grandmother Baekju's only daughter named Wise Girl.

She was more beautiful and ravishing than all the fairies in Cheonjiwang's heavenly home. After seeking permission, he married Wise Girl, and she became known as Wise Wife. He stayed with his new wife for four days and nights and then left. But before he left, Cheonjiwang gave his wife two gourd seeds. He also told her to name their children "Small Star" and "Great Star." He then rode away to the heavens in his golden chariot.

Wise Girl gave birth to twin boys and named them according to her husband's wishes. When the children were old enough to understand, they wanted to know their father's identity. Wise Wife revealed that their father was Cheonjiwang. Again, according to their father's wishes, they sowed seeds, and long vines grew from them, rising to the heavens until they reached the throne of the leader of the Gods. The vines grew around and entwined the left armrest of the throne.

The twin boys then started climbing the vines. However, due to their weight, the armrest broke. From that event and onwards, thrones did not have the left armrest. Cheonjiwang just needed one glance to confirm that the twin boys were his sons. He then ordered a contest between his sons to decide which brother would help him rule the heavens, the human world, and the earth, because he found it exceedingly difficult to manage them all alone.

The first contest was based on riddles. The rule for this contest was simple. Great Star was to ask his brother two riddles. If Small Star got the answers right, he would rule over the mortal world, and Great Star would be the ruler of the nether world. If Small Star gave the wrong answers, their roles would be reversed.

The first riddle from Great Star to his brother was this, "Why do the leaves of some trees fall while those of other trees do not?" Small Star's answer was, "The trees with hollow leaves were shed while those leaves which were full and not hollow did not fall." Great Star countered this answer by showing trees with full leaves that shed too.

The second riddle of Great Star was this, "Which plants grow better? The ones in the higher regions or those in the lower regions?" Small Star said that the plants in the lower regions grew better. His brother was able to refute this too with this counterargument, "The hair on the head (higher regions) grew better than the hair on the feet (lower regions)." So, the Great Star won the contest and was chosen to rule the mortal world.

However, the Small Star was not happy about living in the underworld. So, he pleaded to have a second contest to decide the winner. His brother agreed, and their father came up with another competition.

So, the second contest was to grow flowers for a hundred days. The leader of the gods gave each of his sons a pot and seeds. The one whose flowers were better would rule the mortal world, and the other brother would rule the underworld.

Great Star's flowers blossomed fully and beautifully, while Small Star's flowers dried out and died. As days passed, it was clear as to who would emerge the winner. But, the day before the end of the contest, Small Star secretly switched his plant with his brother's. He declared himself the winner the next day, and wrongfully his brother had to go to the underworld.

As soon as he was made ruler of the mortal world, Small Star invaded Sumyeong Jangja, defeated him, and captured his beasts and animals. He forced Jangja to kneel before him. He then ordered his men to tear the defeated king's body into four parts and fling the dismembered flesh and bones into the air. Jangja's bones and flesh turned into swarms of pests, mosquitoes, bed bugs, and flies, which explains how we still have these very same pests plaguing us today.

Not satisfied with killing Sumyeong Jangja, the bloodthirsty Small Star killed his children too. Jangja's son turned into a kite while his daughter became a bean weevil. The evil Small Star razed Jangja's palace too. Immediately after the cruel execution, catastrophic changes took place in the mortal world.

All living things, including beasts, plants, grasses, fish, birds, etc., suddenly were able to speak and shout, and loudness was the order of the day. The mortal world became extremely loud. When human beings tried to talk to each other, there was chaos because gwisins (or ghosts) participated in the conversation. For example, if a human asked a fellow human a question, then it would be answered by a ghost and not the person to whom the question was put.

Also, thanks to the two suns and moons, many human beings burned in the intense heat during the day and froze to death at night. All these problems drove human beings to lead lives of immorality filled with aggressiveness, promiscuity, and injustice. People resorted to lying and trickery for survival.

Small Star became overwhelmed with all that he had to contend with and had no option but to seek the help of his brother, Great Star, who readily offered help to get rid of the chaos and mayhem. The first thing to get done was to reduce the intensity of the heat and cold. For this, Great Star used his two powerful arrows called Cheongeunsal, each weighing a massive 600 kilograms. He also got five sacks of pine dust ready.

He shot the first Cheongeunsal and destroyed one of the two suns. The residual dust from this destroyed the sun and became the stars of the eastern sky. He shot the second arrow and destroyed one of the two moons, and the residual dust became stars of the western sky. After this incident, there remained only one sun, one moon, and innumerable stars in the sky.

Great Star then sprinkled all the pine dust on the moral world. When this dust came in contact with a beast, plant, or any other non-human form of life, it lost its power of speech. And lastly, he sorted out the problem of gwisins. All the lightweight beings became ghosts, and the heavy beings became human. After finishing the tasks successfully, Great Star returned to his home in the netherworld.

In the confusion, Small Star forgot to mention the immoral behaviors of human beings, which is why betrayal, promiscuity, etc., continue to plague us. Small Star did not have the strength to do anything about it, and these chaotic human habits remain to this day.

Wise Wife became Bajiwang or the earth goddess. The four realms in the cosmos, including the heavens, netherworld, mortal world, and the earth, came to have a ruler each.

Chapter 4: Mythical Creatures and Mountain Spirits

The Korean folklore and mythology realm are filled with magical and mystical creatures and spirits. Let us look at some of them here.

Mythical Creatures

Bulgasari

This is an unusual hybrid creature. The literal translation of the word "bulgasari" is "that which cannot be killed." It is described as a frightening monster that ate up all the metal scraps on which it could lay its hands. People tried different ways to destroy and kill the bulgasari, but their efforts failed.

Some scholars translate the word as "only can be killed by fire" because fire is the only weakness the bulgasari had. Even so, if it is thrown into a fire, it emerges from the fire, its body fully aflame, and burns everything it touches. The hybrid creature has the following parts:

- The body of a bear covered with needle furs.

- The nose of an elephant.

- The eyes of a rhino.

- The claws of a tiger.

- The tail of a bull.

The most common explanation for the origin of the bulgasari is that it was created by a Buddhist monk using rice paste. The mythological story of its origin goes something like this. One day, the government passed an order to round up and arrest all the Buddhist monks in the region. All the monks tried to escape, but one of them sought shelter with his sister, who hid him in her closet.

However, the sister had other plans. She called her husband and told him to report her brother to the government authorities in return for a nice reward. Her husband was so angry with his wife for betraying her brother that he killed her. He then set the monk free.

While the monk was hiding in the closet, he made a grotesque figurine with the steamed rice his sister had given him to eat. The monk fed this figurine with some needles he found in the closet. Strangely, the object ate up all the needles and came out of the closet, looking for other metal scraps. With each meal of metal scrap, the object grew in size until it became a metal-eating bulgasari.

Dokkaebi

These are goblins with devil-like faces and features and are known to cause a lot of mischief. Dokkaebi like to live in isolated areas such as the deep wilderness and/or cemeteries.

This mischievous creature enjoys playing pranks and practical jokes while rewarding good people and punishing bad ones. They love to challenge anyone to a game of ssireum, a popular form of wrestling in Korea. The trick to defeating a dokkaebi is to push at it from its right side, as they are very strong from the left side. It is possible to defeat a dokkaebi by hooking its leg as it only has one.

A dokkaebi also owns many magical tools and items, including:

- Gamtu - The hat of invisibility. This tool helps them vanish when they need to.

- Bangmangi - A spiked club used to punish sinners and to summon things magically.

Dragons

While some features of dragons in Korean mythology are similar to those that appear in Chinese mythology, they have some distinctive Korean concepts not found in any other mythology. Korean dragons do not represent fire. They stand for water and agriculture. They are believed to have the power to summon clouds and rain.

Korean dragons lived in water bodies and were very helpful to human beings. Some dragons even felt complex emotions like human beings. Korean dragons are depicted holding an orb called Yeouiju. This all-powerful orb granted omnipotence to the holder, thereby demonstrating the limitless powers of Korean dragons.

There are four-clawed and three-clawed Korean dragons. Only the four-clawed dragons had an orb because the three-clawed ones could not hold it. In Korean mythology, the precursors of dragons are imugi, a serpent-like creature. When an imugi catches a Yeouiju that fell from the heavens, it becomes a dragon.

Gwisin

In Korean mythology, gwisins are generally ghosts of people who have died. Gwisins are also called Yogoe and are restless souls of the dead who refuse to pass on to the underworld. The reasons for this are most likely because they have not completed their allotted tasks in the mortal world. The presence of gwisin is often depicted with an eerie feeling such as an inexplicable cold sensation, the feel of a light breeze, etc.

These mythical creatures are commonly depicted as women wearing long, flowing white funerary garments and long, black, flowing hair representing the departed soul of a maiden whose task in the mortal world remains incomplete. Gwisins are of different types, including:

- Cheonyeo Gwisin – The most commonly depicted gwisins are long-haired women wearing white robes. They are harmful female ghosts.

- Mool Gwisin or Water Ghost - A ghost representing the soul of a drowning victim. Sometimes spelled as "mul," these gwisins live in water and believe that they are still living. They swim towards living people seeking their help.

- Mongdal Gwisin - The ghost of a bachelor.

- Dalgyal Gwisin or Egg Ghost - Ghost depicted with the head of an egg instead of a face. Normal facial features are replaced by smooth skin. They do not have descendants, and therefore, any signs of humanity is stripped from them.

Bonghwang

This mythical bird appears in nearly all Southeast Asian myths and legends and controls and dominates all other birds. It is often compared to the mythical phoenix of western mythology. In Korean mythology, the bonghwang is a hybrid bird that combines the features of the following animals:

- A rooster's beak.

- A swallow's face.

- A fowl's forehead.

- A snake's head.

- A goose's breast.

- A tortoise's back.

- A stag's backside.

- A fish's tail.

Chollima

Like Pegasus in Greek mythology, the chollima is a high-speed winged horse believed to run and/or fly extremely fast. It is believed to be able to run about 400 kilometers in one day. Interestingly, this distance is the same as the length of the entire Korean peninsula. According to Korean mythology, this winged horse wanted to be domesticated. However, no one had the strength to tame this powerful horse. Therefore, the chollima flew up far into the sky.

Gumiho

Also spelled kumijo, the gumiho is a mythical nine-tailed fox endowed with a lifespan of a thousand years. At the end of its 1000-year life, a gumiho obtains shape-shifting powers and can transform itself into any shape, although most often, choosing to become a beautiful woman who seduces men so they can eat their heart and liver. In some Korean versions, gumiho are shown as half-fox, half-human bloodthirsty creatures wandering around in cemeteries and graveyards.

Haechi

Also known as Haitai or Haetae, this mythical creature was half-lion and half-watchdog. It also had a horn in the center of its head. Its food is fire, and it symbolizes justice. It is known to offer protection against fire-related natural disasters and against disruptive changes and is therefore placed in front of homes and buildings.

Samjoko

This three-legged crow was a symbol of power during the rule of the Goguryeo Dynasty. In fact, it was considered to be more powerful than dragons and bonghwangs. Samjoko is believed to live in the sun and, therefore, represents the sun's power. There are several famous folklore stories about this mythical creature.

The original name of Mount Geumo was Mount Daebon, the Great Roots Mountain. A Chinese envoy from the Tang dynasty saw an iridescent bird in the sky, and completely enamored by its colors and beauty, he followed it. Little did the envoy know that this was samjoko and it led him to Mount Daebon, where he simply disappeared. From then on, Mount Daebon was called Geuma, or Golden Crow (gold signifies sun).

Another legend tells the story of how samjoko is connected to the sun. There lived a couple named Yeono and Seo in the Silla Kingdom during the rule of King Adalla. One day, this couple sat on a floating rock and went away to

Japan, where they were crowned king and queen. Meanwhile, in Silla, sunlight and moonlight disappeared.

Experts were called to find out the reason. They said that Silla is in darkness because the sun's and moon's energy represented by Yeono and Seo have gone away. King Adalla sent an emissary to Japan requesting them to come back. But they responded that if King Adalla performed a ritual using the silk fabric woven by Seo, then the light from the sun and moon would return. The ritual was performed, and light returned to Silla. The couple's names have the Chinese character 烏, which translates to "crow."

Mountain Spirits in Korean Mythology

San-shin or mountain spirits appear in numerous Korean folklore. Here are some interesting and popular myths and legends.

The Story of Yeonjin

Many eons ago, a childless old couple named Yeonjin, and Hoya lived in the Great Sage Scenic Valley (Daeseong Gyegok in the Korean language) in Mount Jiri. The couple yearned for a child. One day, a bear approached Yeonjin and told her about a magical secret spring in Mount

Jiri. The Yin-Yang spring was known to help childless couples have children.

Yeonjin was so excited to hear about this water source that she decided to visit the place and try her luck immediately, without even pausing to speak to her husband about it. Now, a tiger from the mountain, which was the bear's rival, reported this conversation he had overheard to the mountain spirit (san-shin) of Mount Jiri.

The goddess of Mount Jiri was angry with the bear for revealing such important secrets to human beings. So, she imprisoned the bear in a cave. As a reward for reporting the incident, the tiger was made "King of the Jungle." Jiri-san-shin punished Yeojin for stealing holy water from the sacred spring. Yeojin was sentenced to cultivate azalea flowers on Seseok-pyeong-jeon, a rocky plateau, for the rest of her life.

It was not an easy task growing flowers on a rocky plateau. But Yeonjin had no choice but to fulfill her punishment. She worked so hard that her body was completely worn out. It is believed that the unfortunate Yeonjin blood from her worn fingers fell on the flowers, which helped them bloom. This is the reason for the deep scarlet color of azalea flowers. Even today, it is believed that azaleas hold the soul of Yeonjin.

Yeonjin regretted her mistakes and prayed for forgiveness to the mountain goddess of Cheon-Hwang-bong, the Heavenly Peak, the highest mountain in mainland South Korea. She lit candles facing this mountain and prayed for mercy every day during the last days of her life. When she died, Yeonjin was transformed into a boulder.

The Story of Benevolent Gari-Wang-San-Shin

Gari-wang-san, the King of Universe Mountain (located in present-day Gangwon Province), is one of the highest peaks in Korea. Many centuries ago, the mother of a good family living on the western side of this peak caught a deadly disease. The local physician said that only a particular fish found on the eastern coast could heal her. Sadly, no one had the courage or means to undertake the dangerous journey.

But the lady's oldest son decided to go because he was determined to save his mother. The journey was long, arduous, and fraught with danger. When he reached a high mountain pass, a tiger suddenly confronted him. Terrified, the son thought that he would be killed, but the tiger simply knelt down on the ground and told the boy to climb on its back. It sped off rapidly and reached the coast where the boy could catch that special fish.

The tiger then took him back and left him close to his house. At the end of the journey, the tiger revealed itself as Gari-wang-san-shin, the mountain spirit of Gari-wang-san. Korean folklore and myths reveal both the punishing and rewarding sides of deities, gods, and goddesses.

Chapter 5: The Three Ancient Korean Kingdoms

In Korea, founding myths are called Geonguksinhwa and are considered sacred stories regarding the origin of their nation. Founding myths of Korea are recorded in:

- Dangungogi - Ancient Records of Dangun.

- Samgungnyusa - Memorabilia of the Three Kingdoms.

- Goguryeo Bongi - The Records of Goguryeo.

These myths are also found as a separate section titled "The History of the Three Kingdoms" in the Samguk Sagi. The ancient Three Kingdoms including Goguryeo, Silla, and Baekje, were later unified to become the present-day Korean peninsula.

The ancient founding myths of Korea all have several similar characteristics. First, there is always a sacred union between gods, goddesses, and divine deities. Dangun of Gojoseon was born to Hwanung and Ungneyo. Jumong of Goguryeo was born to Yuhwa and Haemosu. In Silla,

Hyeokgeose was the male deity, and Alyeong was the female deity.

The brides are goddesses and female deities of Mother Earth, and the grooms are gods and male deities of the heavens. Let us look at each of these three kingdoms in a bit of detail:

Founding of Silla

Silla was in the southeastern part of the Korean Peninsula. Korean mythological folklore says that King Bak Hyeokgeose hatched out of an egg laid by a chicken-dragon. He is believed to be the ancestor of those with Park or Bak as their family name. Before Bak Hyeokgeose came into existence, the people of the six villages of Gyeongju, had their own leaders but no king.

The people decided they needed an overlord because otherwise, governing the villages would not be possible. They went in search of a virtuous man to be their king. They went from place to place until eventually, the people saw the light near a well. As they approached the light, they saw a strange sight. A horse was bowing near the light.

When the people went even closer, the horse rose into the sky and disappeared. In its place was a very large egg which broke as soon as they touched it. A young boy hatched from the broken egg. The bird and animals danced joyfully at the sight of the young boy. All the villagers realized this was a sign from the heavens. Their gods had sent them a divine king. They named the boy Bak Hyeokgeose. Bak means egg, and Hyeokgeose means "the one who will rule with the bright light."

They raised him to become a king, and when he turned thirteen, the villagers looked for a suitable wife for him. Alyeong was sent from the heavens to become the first queen of Silla. On the same day, another strange thing happened in the village of Saryang. A unique animal called a kyeryong, a cross between a dragon and a chicken, appeared near a well. A baby girl was born from the left side of this animal. Although she was a beautiful baby, she also had a beak like that of a chicken.

However, when the villagers took the baby for a bath, the beak fell off. The villagers named her after the Aleyong well, near where she had been found. They carried the girl and raised her. She was married to Bak at the age of thirteen, after which they were crown king and queen of Silla. Bak ruled for 61 years and ascended to heaven when his time came.

Of the three kingdoms, Silla is credited with bringing about the unification of Korea. It was also known for its excellent art and culture. Silla allowed Buddhism to flourish so that it spread to the entire Korean peninsula.

Founding of Goguryeo

Goguryeo became the largest kingdom in the whole of Korea. It was established by Jumong, the son of Haemosu and Yuhwa. He is known as the Holy King of the East. Haemosu married Yuhwa against her wishes. After several attempts to escape from her husband, she finally succeeded and found refuge with King Keuma of Puyeo (or Dongbueyo). There, she delivered an egg containing the son of her husband.

Her protector King Keuma tried to destroy it. He prevented Yuhwa from giving the required warmth for the egg to hatch. But it was warmed by the shaft of light that his father, Haemosu, sent. Even on cloudy days, the egg was kept warm and safe. King Keuma placed the egg in his stables among some frighteningly wild horses. However, the horses were not able to trample or destroy it. He then left the egg in the deep parts of the wilderness. Again, no wild animal was able to harm it.

Finally, Keuma gave in and allowed Yuhwa to hatch the egg. When the time came, Jumong, the son of Haemosu, burst forth from it. Jumong's divinity soon became evident. He began to speak within a month of hatching from the egg. He grew incredibly fast and was an adult in no time.

His archery skills were outstandingly good. He could shoot the smallest of objects like little insects and fleas from a distance with amazing accuracy. He grew up along with King Keuma's sons, but he was better than them at everything, which led to the sons resenting Jumong and his outstanding warrior skills. Eventually, this resentment boiled over into open conflict.

Tired of their resentful attitude, Jumong left Keuma's kingdom with his first wife, his mother, and his son. With Yuhwa's blessings, he headed southward to establish his own kingdom. However, one of King Keuma's sons pursued him to try to stop him at the River Kaesa. Jumong used his divine powers to summon all the fish and other water animals and asked them to form a bridge across the river. After he crossed over, the aquatic animals swam away, and the bridge collapsed. All his pursuers fell into the water.

Jumong's next stop was King Songyang. He defeated the king in an archery contest and overthrew him with the help of his sacred bugle and drum. Jumong then called upon Aryongjong, the goddess of rain, to cause flooding in Songyang's capital city. However, he made sure the common people of the city were saved from the floods. He rode a horse-sized duck on the water for this purpose.

When the capital city was completely washed away, Jumong again used his divine powers to create a new city that became the capital of his kingdom, Goguryeo. Jumong went on and conquered the neighboring kingdoms of Biryu, Malgal, Northern Okjeo, and Haengin.

While he was busy establishing a large kingdom, his mother, Yuhwa, who he had left in Puyeo, fell ill and died. When Jumong heard of his mother's passing, he sent for his wife, Ye, and son, Yuri. Yuri was as illustrious as his father. This made Jumong's second wife jealous, and she left him and went southwards along with her sons, Biryu and Onjo, who wanted to establish their own kingdoms.

The Myth of Talhae

Talhae was the fourth king of Silla. He was also the progenitor of the people with the family name "Seok." During the reign of King Namhae, the second Silla ruler, an old fisherwoman named Ajineuiseon saw a strange sight on the seas of Ajinpo. A flock of noisy magpies was following a boat that carried a large chest on its decks

The boat came to the shore, and the old lady opened the chest. Inside it was a young, noble-looking boy. The chest also contained two slaves and plenty of treasure. Ajineuiseon looked after the boy for seven days. Then, he revealed his identity. He said the queen delivered him of Yong Seong Guk, the Dragon Fortress Kingdom.

But since he was born in an egg, she abandoned him in a boat, and that is how he reached near the old fisherwoman. After saying this, he left the lady and went with his slaves and treasure to Mount Toham. There, he dug a tomb and found living quarters in the fortress on that mountain and lived there for seven days.

Talhae then came up with a scheme. He went to the house of Hogong, the high minister and dug a small pit where he buried a whetstone and some charcoal. The next morning, he proclaimed that the high minister's house had belonged to his family for generations. He declared that he had been a blacksmith, and while he was away in foreign lands, Hogong had taken over his family home.

Talhae said that he could prove that this was once a blacksmith's house. He asked the people gathered to dig around the house, and they were certain to find the smithy tools he had buried. Naturally, the royal authorities dug up the whetstone and charcoal. The authorities were then convinced the house belonged to Talhae's family, and so he could take possession of it. The story reached the ears of King Nimhae, who was impressed with the intelligence of the boy and arranged for his oldest daughter to marry him.

Another famous story illustrating Talhae's intelligence and power goes like this. One day, he ordered his slave named White Garment (Baekeui) to get some water from the Yonaejeong well. He warned him not to drink any of the water. However, the slave took a sip of water before reaching Talhae, and the bowl stuck to the slave's lips and would not come off.

He came running to Talhae, apologizing profusely and begging his forgiveness. Only after Talhae gave him a good scolding for not obeying orders did the bowl come off from the slave's lips. Baekeui never tried to deceive Talhae again.

After Nimhae, Norye became king of Silla. After Norye's passing, Talhae ascended the throne and ruled for 23 years. When he died, his body was buried in Socheongu Hills. Later, he appeared as a spirit and commanded that his bones should be dug up. The exhumed bones were very strong and clearly belonged to a powerful man. The bones were crushed and made into a statue of Talhae, which was placed in the palace.

Talhae reappeared again as a spirit and told the people of Silla to enshrine his statue on Dongak. From then on, Talhae was worshiped throughout the kingdom as Dongakshin, the deity of Dongak.

Founding of Baekje

The Baekje Kingdom was established in the southwestern part of the Korean peninsula. Interestingly, only the founding of the Baekje Kingdom does not involve gods and goddesses, as King Onjo established it.

Onjo was the third son of Jumong. Biryu was his older brother. When his father Jumong called for his eldest son from his first wife, Onjo realized his chances of inheriting Goguryeo were less than negligible. So, he decided to move away from his father and set up his own kingdom. His mother agreed to leave her husband and go with her sons, so they moved south.

Onjo decided to set up camp on the banks of the Han River. His older brother, Biryu, wanted to go further southward towards rivers that were closer to the sea. But Onjo built a big fortress which he named Wiryeseong in Hanam, in the eastern part of present-day Seoul. From here, Onjo established his new kingdom, which he named Sipje. "Sip" translates to "ten."

Onjo gave this name to his new kingdom because ten loyal subjects helped him set up his new kingdom. The choice of the location of his empire was perfect because smithies and farming were both highly developed in the areas around the banks of the Han River. His empire was also close enough to the sea that his subjects could accept and assimilate advanced cultures and improved resources coming from kingdoms outside of the Korean peninsula.

The location chosen by Biryu, on the other hand, did not work out well for him. The land was not agri-friendly. Because of its proximity to the sea, it was very salty and this prevented successful crops. When his kingdom did not take off, Biryu came and settled with his younger brother at Wiryeseong. When he died, his territories were annexed by Sipje. At this time, Onjo changed his kingdom's name to Baekje. "Baek" translates to "numerous" or "many." The name of his kingdom contained his hope that many more would join him and his territories would expand.

Onjo's groundwork formed a firm foundation for a great kingdom that contributed to the growth and development of Korea and Japan. The Baekje Kingdom lasted for nearly seven centuries and was ruled by 31 kings until 660 AD when it was conquered by joint forces of Silla and the Chinese Tang dynasty.

Conclusion

That seemingly inexplicable superstitions and myths impact how people in modern-day Korea think still holds true to this day. For example, there is a widespread belief among Koreans that sleeping in a closed room with a fan on can result in death. No one knows how and why this superstition came into being, and many put it down to the influence of myths and ancient legends.

That is what myths and legends do to humans. The lessons they teach can be so deeply ingrained in our psyche that they get embedded into our genetic material and get passed onto future generations. While this superstition might seem silly (in the absence of a valid explanation), there are multiple excellent life lessons that stories in Korean mythology and folklore teach us.

Reading Korean mythology gives us insight into the country's history. We can understand how the myths, legends, and folklore blend into facts, with a bit of magical beauty, added, enriches, and explains a beautiful culture.

References

""Alyeong | Facts, Information, and Mythology." ."
Pantheon.org, pantheon.org/articles/a/alyeong.html.

""Bak Hyeokgeose | Facts, Information, and Mythology." ."
Pantheon.org,
pantheon.org/articles/b/bak_hyeokgeose.html.

""Folk-Stories about Korean San-Shin." ." Www.san-
Shin.org, www.san-shin.org/stories1.html.

국립민속박물관. ""Founding Myth." ." Encyclopedia of
Korean Folk Culture, 2019,
folkency.nfm.go.kr/en/topic/detail/5324.

---. ""Impossible-To-Kill." ." Encyclopedia of Korean Folk
Culture, 2022, folkency.nfm.go.kr/en/topic/detail/5534#.

---. ""Legends of Place Names." ." Encyclopedia of Korean
Folk Culture, 2022,
folkency.nfm.go.kr/en/topic/detail/5665.

---. ""Myth of Dangun." ." Encyclopedia of Korean Folk
Culture, 2019, folkency.nfm.go.kr/en/topic/detail/5336.

---. ""Myth of Haemosu." ." Encyclopedia of Korean Folk
Culture, 2022, folkency.nfm.go.kr/en/topic/detail/5414.

---. ""Myth of Seok Talhae." ." Encyclopedia of Korean
Folk Culture, 2022,
folkency.nfm.go.kr/en/topic/detail/5360.

---. ""Origin of Seven Stars." ." Encyclopedia of Korean
Folk Culture, 2022,
folkency.nfm.go.kr/en/topic/detail/5408.

---. ""Song of the Creation of the Universe." ."
Encyclopedia of Korean Folk Culture, 2019,
folkency.nfm.go.kr/en/topic/detail/5402.

---. ""Three-Legged Crow." ." Encyclopedia of Korean Folk
Culture, 2022, folkency.nfm.go.kr/en/topic/detail/5550.

"King Onjo." World.kbs.co.kr,
world.kbs.co.kr/service/contents_view.htm?menu_cate=
history&board_seq=4031&page=0.

""Korean Creation." ." Mythpedia Wiki,
mythpedia.fandom.com/wiki/Korean_Creation#Jeju_Isla
nd_Version.

Service (KOCIS), Korean Culture and Information.
""Jumong: Founder of Goguryeo Kingdom Is Man of
Legend, History : Korea.net : The Official Website of the
Republic of Korea." ." Www.korea.net,
www.korea.net/NewsFocus/Culture/view?articleId=12157
2.

---. ""Pak Hyeokgeose: The Founder of the Silla Kingdom
Was Respected and Courageous : Korea.net : The Official
Website of the Republic of Korea." ." Www.korea.net,
www.korea.net/NewsFocus/Culture/view?articleId=12186
6&fbclid=IwAR3M2cOvvQTkTSm7fUiL7GfQrqIqxfkwW1k
00ECgd25y6tTgwSohYUsdsoY.

Supernatural Creatures of Korean Mythology.
koreanetblog.blogspot.com/2011/12/supernatural-
creatures-of-korean.html.

""The Caligula." ." TV Tropes,
tvtropes.org/pmwiki/pmwiki.php/Main/TheCaligula.

"'"THE TOP 11 DEITIES in KOREAN MYTHOLOGY."
Balladeer's Blog, Balladeer's Blog, 4 June 2016,
glitternight.com/2011/03/24/the-top-11-deities-in-
korean-mythology/.

"Yeongdeung Halmang, Goddess of Wind and Sea - JEJU
WEEKLY." Www.jejuweekly.com,
www.jejuweekly.com/news/articleView.html?idxno=3036
.

Printed in Great Britain
by Amazon

27983396R00046